Active Training for Reading and Writing through 15 Topics

読む力、書く力をつける 15 トピックのアクティブ・トレーニング

by
Michael Schauerte
Tom Dillon
Koji Nishiya

TSURUMI SHOTEN

画像クレジット一覧

Unit 1: ©Monet—Fotolia
Unit 2: ©mimon—Fotolia
Unit 3: ©beeboys—Fotolia
Unit 4: ©Petrafler Ltd—Fotolia
Unit 5: （左）©rook76—Fotolia　（右）©laufer—Fotolia
Unit 6: ©kamichou—Fotolia
Unit 7: ©Monet—Fotolia
Unit 8: ©kamichou—Fotolia
Unit 9: ©feathercollector—Fotolia
Unit 10: ©Rob Hill—Fotolia
Unit 11: ©WWW.SERKAT.AT—Fotolia
Unit 12: ©Stockr—Fotolia
Unit 13: ©Africa Studio—Fotolia
Unit 14: ©aguadeluna—Fotolia
Unit 15: ©Juergen Philipps—Fotolia
表紙　　©Africa Studio—Fotolia

はしがき

　インターネットをとおして、いろいろな情報を検索したり、英語のサイトを閲覧する機会が増えています。Yahoo, Wikipedia, Google などの検索で記事やニュースを見ることができますし、Facebook や Twitter でも世界中がつながっています。日本人の立場から考えると、膨大な英語の情報が氾濫して、一歩間違えるとその洪水に溺れる危険性もありますが、知りたいことを効率的に的確に取得したり、また、これまで知らなかったことや人に出会い、自分の世界が豊かになる可能性も広がっているのです。

　本書は、このような可能性を自分のものにするために、英語の文章を理解するスキルを伸ばす教材として企画されました。素材としては、様ざまなテーマの英文を350語程度から400語程度のパッセージにまとめ、豊富なトレーニングを取り入れました。特に、トピックを捉えるトレーニング、パラグラフの構造を捉えるトレーニングを中心に、Comprehension Questions、内容要約、さらに、英作文まで、豊富なトレーニングがアクティブにできるように工夫してあります。

　素材となる英文は、しっかりした構成の英文作成に豊富な経験と実績のあるトム・ディロン氏とマイケル・シャワティー氏と一緒に、テーマの選定・執筆からエクササイズの作成まで、入念な打ち合わせを重ねた結果できあがったものです。

　本書を執筆するにあたり、様ざまなジャンルからバラエティに富んだトピックの英文を作成していただいたマイケル・シャワティー氏・トム・ディロン氏にあらためて心からお礼申し上げます。

　本書を通じて、英文を読むスキルが格段に向上し、さらに、英語をとおして知識・情報を得るだけでなく、自身の世界と、また、世界とのつながりが豊かになることの一助になれば、著者としても大きな喜びです。

2015 年 10 月

著者代表　西谷恒志

CONTENTS

Unit 1　**Health**　○怖いドライアイ○
　　　　Dry Eye Syndrome 1

Unit 2　**Culture**　○フランス人は映画好き○
　　　　French Are Fond of Films 6

Unit 3　**History**　○アルファベットのはじまり○
　　　　The ABCs of the Alphabet 11

Unit 4　**Biography**　○サッカーのレジェンド、ペレ○
　　　　Brazil's Soccer Legend Pelé 16

Unit 5　**Literature**　○フィッツジェラルドとヘミングウェイ○
　　　　Friends and Rivals 21

Unit 6　**Tourism**　○中国からの旅行者○
　　　　Chinese Overseas 26

Unit 7　**Social Problems**　○スマホ依存症○
　　　　Loving Your Smartphone (Too Much) 31

Unit 8　**Sociology**　○高齢社会と向き合う○
　　　　Dealing with the Graying Population 36

Unit 9　**Animals**　○金色の毒ガエル○
　　　　Golden Poison Frog 41

Unit 10　**Art**　○シェイカー教徒の手づくり家具○
　　　　Shaker Furniture 46

Unit 11　**Food**　○夢の食品、チア・シード○
　　　　Chia Seeds—the Super Food 51

Unit 12　**Science/Technology**　○ドローンの平和的利用法○
　　　　Drones 56

Unit 13　**Language**　○Nice! 昔の意味は Not nice!○
　　　　How Words Can Change 61

Unit 14　**Psychology**　○15歳も50歳も大変○
　　　　It's Not Easy Being 15 or 50 66

Unit 15　**Sports**　○カーリング・ストーンのトリビア○
　　　　Curling Stones 71

各ユニットの構成と利用法

15 ユニットの中に、豊富なジャンルとトピックの英文が入っています。

★ Keywords
キーとなる単語・熟語：マッチングの問題形式。
最低限必要なものですから、クラスのレベルに応じて、項目を追加していただければと思います。

★ 英文
豊富なジャンルから様ざまなトピックを選びました。学習者の興味が持続します。
英文を読み始める前に、必ずユニット冒頭の説明文を読ませてください。英文の理解度が確実に上がります。

★ Exercises 1
英文の構成理解。ディスコース・マーカー中心に。
問題を解くことで、パッセージを構成するパラグラフ間の関係や、論理の流れが理解できます。

★ Exercises 2
トピックセンテンス（主題文）の理解
パッセージの全体的な理解のあと、本文全体のトピックセンテンス（主題文）を指摘させて、パッセージの主題を確認させます。

★ Exercises 3
Comprehension Questions: 2 問
パッセージの内容に関して、全体的なことを問う質問と、具体的な情報を問う質問です。

★ Exercises 4
True-False: 3 問
パッセージの内容に一致しているかどうかを問う問題です。

★ Exercises 5
内容要約文完成と空所補充問題
センテンスを並べ替えてパッセージの要約文を完成させる問題です。空所補充問題を兼ねます。

★ Exercises 6
部分英作文
パッセージに出てくる語句をターゲットにした問題。必要に応じてヒントをふやしてください。

Unit 1 Health

怖いドライアイ

Dry Eye Syndrome

ドライアイは目の疾患の一つで、涙の量が少なくなったり、質が低下したりすることで眼の表面を潤す力が低下する。原因は様ざまで、加齢、PCのモニターやスマートフォンの画面の見過ぎ、乾燥した環境（冬の乾燥、エアコン使用による部屋の乾燥）、コンタクトレンズの使用などがある。目の乾燥感だけでなく、異物感、痛み、まぶしさ、目の疲れなどが続いたときはドライアイを疑う必要がある。

Keywords

本文に使われている次の語句の意味としてもっとも適切なものを a〜j から選びなさい。

1. (l.4) irritating	a. さらす [さらされる] こと	1. ( )
2. (l.5) syndrome	b. 点眼液、目薬	2. ( )
3. (l.8) moist	c. 熱中者、大ファン	3. ( )
4. (l.10) exposure	d. 加湿器	4. ( )
5. (l.17) redden	e. 症候群	5. ( )
6. (l.21) over-the-counter	f. 〜するよう努力する	6. ( )
7. (l.21) eye drops	g. 赤くなる	7. ( )
8. (l.22) humidifier	h. （目が）潤った	8. ( )
9. (l.22) addict	i. 市販の	9. ( )
10. (l.28) strive to *do*	j. イライラさせる、悩ましい	10. ( )

Unit 1　Health

　　The rapid growth of the Internet has led to more than an increased ease in communication and a worldwide spread of information. The hours and hours that many people now spend staring at computers and smartphones have also created a new wave of an irritating health problem known as "Dry Eye Syndrome."

　　Dry Eye Syndrome occurs when the eye does not receive enough moisture. Blinking covers the surface of the eye with a thin layer of tears and this keeps most eyes moist, with the average person blinking around fifteen times per minute. In the past, the more common causes for Dry Eye Syndrome included over-usage of contact lenses, too much exposure to windy weather or just natural aging. (　A　), eyes can receive less moisture than needed. Yet, these days prolonged concentration before a computer can lead to decreased blinking and thus fewer tears around the eyes. The result is that modern man is suffering from Dry Eye Syndrome more than ever.

　　While uncomfortable, Dry Eye Syndrome is typically not so serious. Those who suffer from the syndrome may feel as if their eyes are somewhat burning. They may rub their eyes frequently and their eyes may redden as a result. (　B　), those with Dry Eye Syndrome may have unclear vision. (　C　), those with the syndrome may feel sensitive to bright light.

　　When Dry Eye Syndrome becomes severe, sufferers should seek medical care. However, most cases can be corrected by over-the-counter eye drops or by the steady use of a humidifier. Yet, for Internet addicts, there is an even easier method. Take a break and turn the computer off! Time away from the computer screen will allow the eye to regain moisture all by itself.

　　Dry Eye Syndrome has become an annoying consequence of humankind's new reliance on computers. While computers have been designed for human convenience, our eyes have not been designed for computers. Computer users should remember this and strive to keep their eyes fresh and rested.

(338 words)

Dry Eye Syndrome

Exercises

1 本文中の空欄（ A ），（ B ），（ C ）に入る語句として最も適切なものを下の①〜③の中から選びなさい。

(A) _____
(B) _____
(C) _____

> ① In other cases
> ② In some cases
> ③ In each case

2 本文全体のトピックセンテンス（主題文）を探して、該当する英文に下線を引きなさい。

3 質問を読み、正しい答を (A) 〜 (D) の中から選びなさい。

Question 1

What is the main idea of this passage?

(A) Staring at a computer screen has caused increased blinking and more cases of Dry Eye Syndrome.
(B) Dry Eye Syndrome is uncomfortable but not so serious.
(C) Staring at a computer screen is an irritating health problem.
(D) Staring at a computer screen has lead to less blinking and more cases of Dry Eye Syndrome.

Question 2

In the pre-Internet days, which of the following individuals might be more likely to suffer from Dry Eye Syndrome?

(A) An elderly person
(B) An average person
(C) A person who rubbed his or her eyes
(D) A person with unclear vision

Unit 1 Health

4 次の英文は本文の内容に関するものである。本文の内容に一致する場合はTを、一致しない場合はFを下線部に記入しなさい。

(a) Dry Eye Syndrome is usually a serious medical condition.
_____

(b) Most people blink about once every four seconds.
_____

(c) People with Dry Eye Syndrome may prefer darkened rooms.
_____

5 a. に続く b. c. d. の英文を正しく並べ替えて本文の要約文を完成させ、正しい順序を下線部に記入しなさい。また、空欄（ A),(B),(C ）に入る最も適切な語句を①〜③の中から選びなさい。

a. Dry Eye Syndrome is on the increase (A) humankind's overuse of computers.
_____

b. The condition can be easily treated, (B) the simplest method is just to spend less time before a computer.

c. The syndrome occurs (C) computer users may not blink enough to properly moisturize their eyes.

d. This will help the eye recover on its own.

正しい順序 a → _____ → _____ → _____

(A) _____ (B) _____ (C) _____

① because
② but
③ due to

6 空欄に適切な単語を書き入れて英訳文を完成させなさい。アルファベットが与えられている場合はその文字で始めること。

(a) 子供たちにとって、異なる種類の考え方にさらされることは大切だ。

It is important for children to have (ex_____) (t_____) different kinds of ideas.

(b) その販売計画によって、社内に新たな部署が創設された。

The sales plan (l_____) (t_____) the creation of a new department in the company.

(c) すべての航空会社は、乗客に対して、帰りのフライトの搭乗確認をオンラインで行わせてくれる。

All airlines (al_____) passengers (t_____) reconfirm their return flights online.

(d) ほとんどの健康保険は、海外旅行中に発生した事故には適用されない。

Most health insurance is not inclusive of accidents that (o_____) (w_____) traveling abroad.

(e) ガソリンが高値なので、今年は車で旅行する人はより少ない。

(F_____) people are traveling by car this year (b_____) (_____) the high gasoline prices.

Unit 2 Culture

フランス人は映画好き

French Are Fond of Films

日本ではフランス映画よりアメリカ映画の方がポピュラーだが、じつは映画は19世紀の終わりにフランスで発明されている。このような理由で映画の創世記においては、フランスの映画技術は世界一であり、また、フランスのPathé社だけで全世界の映画産業の三分の一を支配していた。こうした背景には映画産業に対するフランス政府の手厚い政策があり、そのため現在でもフランス国内で上映される映画の約40％はフランス映画である。

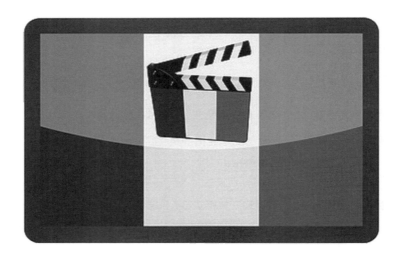

Keywords

本文に使われている次の語句の意味としてもっとも適切なものをa～jから選びなさい。

1. (l.7) policy	a. 貸付金	1. (　　)
2. (l.16) along with	b. 規定数量；割り当て	2. (　　)
3. (l.16) quota [kwóutə]	c. 予算	3. (　　)
4. (l.18) subsidy	d. 収益、収入	4. (　　)
5. (l.19) loan	e. 手段、方策	5. (　　)
6. (l.20) revenue	f. 政策、施策	6. (　　)
7. (l.23) measures	g. 補助金、助成金	7. (　　)
8. (l.24) compete against	h. ～を要求する	8. (　　)
9. (l.24) budget [bʌ́dʒet]	i. ～と競争する	9. (　　)
10. (l.29) demand	j. ～に加えて、～の他に	10. (　　)

French Are Fond of Films

Art and culture have always been important to French people. The French government does many things to protect artistic activities. One example is the French policies toward the national film industry.

Ever since the end of World War II, the French government has tried to protect and promote the production of films in France. In 1948, the government introduced a quota that limited the number of American films that could be shown in France. Around the time that this policy was introduced, roughly 42% of the films shown in France were French films, 44% were American films, and the other films were made in other European countries.

Today, French films still are around 40% of the total film market in France, and American films are about 42% of the total. So it might seem that the French policy did not have much effect on the film market. But if we compare the film industries in other European countries, the influence of the policy becomes clear. This is because in other European countries around (A) of the films that people watch are American films.

Along with quotas, France has protected its film industry in other ways. France requires that at least 40% of TV programs broadcast in the country are produced in France. The French government has also provided subsidies and loans to film producers. The money that the government provides comes from taxes on movie tickets and from revenue from TV stations. The French film industry receives quite a lot of money from these sources.

France has worried about the power of Hollywood. Many French people support the measures to protect French films because they know that it is hard for French films to compete against Hollywood big-budget movies. But at one time, France had the most powerful film industry in the world. In the early years of the film industry until around 1913, one French film production company, Pathé, controlled around a third of the entire global film industry. At that time, it was the American film-producers, not the French, who were demanding that the government provide them with support and protection.

(353 words)

Unit 2   Culture

Exercises

1 本文中の空欄（ A ）に入れるべき適切な数値を次の①〜③より１つ選びなさい。

(A) _____

① 25%
② 40%
③ 65%

2 本文全体のトピックセンテンス（主題文）を探して、該当する英文に下線を引きなさい。

3 質問を読み、正しい答を (A) 〜 (D) の中から選びなさい。

Question 1

What is the main topic of this passage?

(A) The threat of Hollywood to the French film industry
(B) A history of the development of the French film industry
(C) The importance of protecting each country's film industry
(D) The French government's protection of the film industry

Question 2

What happened in 1948?

(A) The number of American films rose quickly to as high as 44%.
(B) Most of the films shown in France were made in other countries.
(C) The French government limited American films in France.
(D) The French government raised the number of French films to around 42%.

4 次の英文は本文の内容に関するものである。本文の内容に一致する場合はTを、一致しない場合はFを下線部に記入しなさい。

(a) There are more American films in other European countries than France.
　_____

(b) The French government provides loans to 40% of TV programs.
　_____

(c) The French film industry used to be stronger than the American film industry.
　_____

5 a. に続く b. c. d. の英文を正しく並べ替えて本文の要約文を完成させ、正しい順序を下線部に記入しなさい。また、空欄（ A ），(B)，(C)に入る最も適切な語句を①〜③の中から選び、必要に応じて正しい活用形に変化させなさい。

a. The French government has been active in protecting the French film industry.

b. The French also (A) their film industry by (B) it with money from taxes and other sources.

c. The French worry about the power of American films, but many years ago the French film industry was the strongest in the world.

d. These efforts date back to the late 1940s, when the government began to (C) the number of American films.

正しい順序　a → _____ → _____ → _____

(A) _____　(B) _____　(C) _____

> ① provide
> ② support
> ③ limit

Unit 2　Culture

6 空欄に適切な単語を書き入れて英訳文を完成させなさい。アルファベットが与えられている場合はその文字で始めること。

(a) 野生動物の生息地を保護するため、政府は多額の費用を使いつづけてきた。

The government has been (s　　　　) a lot of money to (p　　　　) the wildlife habitat.

(b) 社長は就任して最初の週に、全面的な経営変革を導入した。

The president (i　　　　) sweeping managerial (ch　　　　) within his first week of office.

(c) その新しい政策は、子供の面倒を見なければならない父親のために規定を設けている。

The new (p　　　　) makes provisions for fathers who need to (　　　　) for their children.

(d) 技術的な検討をすると、つねに製品の最終設計に影響が出てくる。

Technical considerations always have an (e　　　　) (o　　) the final design of a product.

(e) 減っている学校予算のせいで、ティナは図書館のために資金集めを始めた。

Due to the (d　　　　) school (　　　　), Tina has started fund-raising for the library.

Unit 3　History

アルファベットのはじまり

The ABCs of the Alphabet

> 文字の起源は明らかではないが、紀元前 4000 年頃に使用されたエジプトの壺に象形文字に似たシンボルが描かれている。その後、紀元前 1800 年頃にエジプトで音を表すシンボルを使い始めた。これが初期のアルファベットで、子音を表す文字しかなかったが、その後、この文字がギリシャなどに広がり、母音を表す文字も使用されるようになった。ギリシャ・アルファベットはラテン・アルファベットの基礎となり、現在の英語、フランス語、そして他のヨーロッパ言語につながっている。

Keywords

本文に使われている次の語句の意味としてもっとも適切なものを a～j から選びなさい。

1. (l.3)　take ... for granted
2. (l.5)　creation
3. (l.7)　hieroglyphics [hàiərəglífiks]
4. (l.11)　consonant
5. (l.14)　vowel
6. (l.17)　eventually
7. (l.20)　influential
8. (l.27)　Cyrillic [sərílik]
9. (l.30)　well-suited to
10. (blank)　on the basis of

a. 母音
b. 子音
c. 創造；創作
d. 象形文字
e. ～を特別な注意を払う必要のないものとみなす
f. ～に適した
g. キリル文字の
h. ～に基づいて
i. 結局、やがて
j. 影響力のある

1. (　　)
2. (　　)
3. (　　)
4. (　　)
5. (　　)
6. (　　)
7. (　　)
8. (　　)
9. (　　)
10. (　　)

Unit 3 History

English and many other languages use alphabets for the writing system. For most people, an alphabet is a very normal thing—something that they take for granted. Very few people are aware of the interesting history of how human beings created the first alphabet.

Before the creation of the alphabet, writing systems had been based on symbols to represent things. This was the system used in ancient Egypt, which used a system of symbols called "hieroglyphics." A different symbol was used for each word. Almost 4,000 years ago, around 1800 BC, some people in the area around Egypt began to use these symbols to also represent sounds—rather than just words.

This early alphabet, which had 22 simple symbols to represent consonant sounds, later spread to other areas, including Greece. The Greeks made other changes to the alphabet—keeping some of the symbols and creating other new ones—and they added symbols to also represent vowel sounds. Some experts on the history of the alphabet think that this Greek alphabet was the first "true" alphabet because it made it possible to fully pronounce a word.

At first the Greek alphabet was written from right to left, but eventually they began to write from left to right as people do in European languages today. Several other alphabets were created (A) the Greek Alphabet. The most influential of those alphabets was the Latin alphabet, which is used today for English, French, and many other European languages.

The Latin language was spoken by the Romans in Italy. The Romans created the Latin alphabet by making many changes to the Greek alphabet. The Latin alphabet only had 22 letters, (B) the 26 letters of today's English alphabet.

(C) the Latin alphabet, there are many other alphabets used in the world today, including the Cyrillic alphabet that is used in Russia and other parts of Eastern Europe, and the Arabic alphabet that is used in many parts of the Middle East and North Africa.

All of these alphabets have long histories but they are well-suited to the modern world.

(350 words)

Exercises

1 本文中の空欄（ A),(B),(C)に入る語句として最も適切なものを下の①〜③の中から選びなさい。なお、文頭に来る文字も小文字で表している。

(A) _____
(B) _____
(C) _____

> ① on the basis of
> ② instead of
> ③ in addition to

2 本文全体のトピックセンテンス（主題文）を探して、該当する英文に下線を引きなさい。

3 質問を読み、正しい答を (A) 〜 (D) の中から選びなさい。

Question 1

What is the main topic discussed in this article?

(A) The history of writing systems around the world
(B) The development of the alphabet writing system
(C) A comparison of the Greek and Roman alphabets
(D) An analysis of the best writing systems in the world

Question 2

What is one way that the Greeks changed the alphabet?

(A) They used picture symbols.
(B) They added 22 simple letters.
(C) They began to represent consonant sounds.
(D) They added symbols for the vowel sounds.

Unit 3 History

4 次の英文は本文の内容に関するものである。本文の内容に一致する場合はTを、一致しない場合はFを下線部に記入しなさい。

(a) The first alphabet in the world used symbols called hieroglyphics.
　_____

(b) The Latin alphabet is four words shorter than the English alphabet.
　_____

(c) According to the article, the Latin alphabet was created on the basis of the Greek alphabet.
　_____

5 a. に続くb. c. d. の英文を正しく並べ替えて本文の要約文を完成させ、正しい順序を下線部に記入しなさい。また、空欄（ A),(B),(C) に入る最も適切な語句を①〜③の中から選びなさい。

a. Languages in Europe, the Middle East, and other parts of the world rely on the use of an alphabet for the writing system.
_____

b. (A) had 22 symbols to represent consonant sounds.

c. (B) became the basis for the development of (C) that many European countries use today.

d. This system spread to Greece.

e. The alphabet has a long history, but this writing system is perfectly suited to our modern world.

正しい順序　a → _____ → _____ → _____ → e

(A) _____　(B) _____　(C) _____

```
① the Greek alphabet
② the Latin alphabet
③ the first alphabet
```

6

空欄に適切な単語を書き入れて英訳文を完成させなさい。アルファベットが与えられている場合はその文字で始めること。

(a) 私はタブレットの画面を見るより、本を読む方を好む。

I prefer to read books (r   ) (t   ) looking at tablet's screens.

(b) 歩合はあなたの売上高に応じて支払われる。

Your commission will be paid (b   ) (   ) the amount of sales you make.

(c) 値札にある数字に税金を加えるのをお忘れなく。

Don't forget to (   ) tax (   ) the figure you see on the price tag.

(d) 天気の良い週末を、ゴルフではなく仕事をして過ごすのはあまりうれしくない。

There isn't much happiness in spending a sunny weekend at work (in   ) (   ) golfing.

(e) さらに困ったことに、マークは財布だけでなく車の鍵もなくしてしまった。

In (ad   ) (   ) his troubles, Mark not only lost his wallet but also his car keys.

Unit 4 Biography

サッカーのレジェンド、ペレ

Brazil's Soccer Legend Pelé

ペレは伝説的なサッカー選手で、「サッカーの王様」、あるいは「20世紀最高のサッカー選手」と言われている。彼は15歳でデビューしてから1977年に引退するまでに、1363試合に出場し1281得点を記録しているが、その間、ブラジル代表として3度のワールドカップで優勝している。ペレの影響を受けたと公言している現代の選手としては、ロナウジーニョ、ロベルト・カルロス、ウィントン・ルーファーなど数多くいる。

Keywords

本文に使われている次の語句の意味としてもっとも適切なものを a〜j から選びなさい。

1. (l.3) name *A* after *B*	a. フットボールクラブ	1. ( )
2. (l.5) sock	b. 優勝者の地位	2. ( )
3. (l.8) talented	c. 職業	3. ( )
4. (l.9) FC	d. （得点）を得る	4. ( )
5. (l.10) score	e. （〜することで）終わる	5. ( )
6. (l.12) end up	f. …を〜するように導く	6. ( )
7. (l.12) career	g. 靴下（の片方）	7. ( )
8. (l.14) lead ... to *do*	h. *B* にちなんで *A* に名前を付ける	8. ( )
9. (l.21) at *one's* peak	i. 才能のある	9. ( )
10. (l.23) championship	j. 最高の状態で	10. ( )

One of the most famous soccer players in the history of the sport is Pelé. He was born in Brazil in 1940. Pelé became his nickname, but his real name is Edson Arantes do Nascimento. His parents named him Edson after the American inventor, Thomas Edison. His family was very poor, but his father loved to play soccer and taught his son how to play. The family did not have enough money to buy a soccer ball, so Pelé played with a ball that he made by putting newspapers inside a sock.

(A), it was clear that Pelé was a talented soccer player. In 1956, when he was still just 15 years old, he joined the professional team Santos FC in the city of São Paulo. (B) he was one of the team's best players. He scored his first professional goal in a game played on September 7, 1956. This was the first of the 1,281 goals that he ended up scoring during his professional career.

(C) he became a member of Brazil's national team. In 1958, as a member of the team, he helped lead Brazil to win the World Cup that was held in Sweden. Brazil won the World Cup again four years later, but Pelé was injured in the first game. Brazil's team won another championship with Pelé in 1970 at the World Cup in Mexico.

Pelé played his last season for the team Santos FC in 1974. At first, it seemed he was going to retire from soccer. But two years later, he joined a new team, the New York Cosmos. Even though Pelé could no longer play at his peak, he helped to raise the popularity of soccer in the United States by playing for the team. In 1977, he led the New York Cosmos to the championship of the North American Soccer League.

He played his final match on October 1, 1977, in a game between the Cosmos and Santos FC. Pelé played the first half of the game for the Cosmos, and the second half for his old team Santos FC.

(353 words)

Unit 4　Biography

Exercises

1　本文中の空欄（ A ），(B), (C) に入る語句として最も適切なものを下の①～③の中から選びなさい。

(A) _____
(B) _____
(C) _____

> ① Soon
> ② The next year
> ③ Already as a boy

2　本文全体のトピックセンテンス（主題文）を探して、該当する英文に下線を引きなさい。

3　質問を読み、正しい答を (A) ～ (D) の中から選びなさい。

Question 1

What is the main topic discussed in this article?

(A) Pelé's soccer team Santos FC
(B) Pelé's childhood poverty in Brazil
(C) The professional soccer career of Pelé
(D) The ways in which Pelé changed the game of soccer

Question 2

What happened in 1974?

(A) Pelé participated in his final World Cup.
(B) Pelé played his last season for Santos FC.
(C) Pelé retired from playing soccer professionally.
(D) Pelé became the coach of the New York Cosmos.

Brazil's Soccer Legend Pelé

4 次の英文は本文の内容に関するものである。本文の内容に一致する場合はTを、一致しない場合はFを下線部に記入しなさい。

(a) Pelé was nicknamed "Edson" as a boy.
 _____

(b) Pelé was still a teenager when he became a professional soccer player.
 _____

(c) During Pelé's final soccer game, he played for both teams.
 _____

5 a. に続くb. c. d. の英文を正しく並べ替えて本文の要約文を完成させ、正しい順序を下線部に記入しなさい。また、空欄（ A),(B),(C) に入る最も適切な語句を①〜③の中から選び、必要に応じて正しい活用形に変化させなさい。

a. The famous soccer player Pelé was born in Brazil and started (　A　) professional soccer at the young age of 15.
_____

b. He also (　B　) his soccer teams Santos FC and the New York Cosmos to several championships.

c. He finally retired from professional soccer in 1977.

d. In 1958, he (　C　) Brazil's national team win the World Cup. In total, the Brazil team won the World Cup three times with Pelé.

正しい順序　a → _____ → _____ → _____

(A) _____　(B) _____　(C) _____

① lead
② play
③ help

Unit 4　Biography

6 空欄に適切な単語を書き入れて英訳文を完成させなさい。アルファベットが与えられている場合はその文字で始めること。

(a) 成功している企業は、常に有能な人材を採用しようとしている。

Successful companies are always looking (t　　) hire (t　　　) people.

(b) 仕事の後、よろしかったらあなたも私たちと一緒にビールを1杯飲みましょう。

You're welcome to (j　　　) us after work (f　　　) a beer.

(c) そのサッカーの試合でタイムが告げられたのは、まさにニックが得点を入れようとしていた時だった。

Nick was just about to (　　　　) when time was (c　　　　) in the soccer game.

(d) ケリーは大学の経理部門で会計士としての仕事を始めたところだ。

Kelly has just started her (c　　　　) as an (a　　　　　) in the university's controller's office.

(e) 現在の社長が引退する際には、上席副社長のうちの一人が後任になる。

One of the senior vice-presidents will take over when the (c　　　　) president (r　　　　).

Unit 5 Literature　フィッツジェラルドとヘミングウェイ

Friends and Rivals

> フィッツジェラルドもヘミングウェイも 20 世紀アメリカを代表する作家であるが、この二人は 1925 年にパリで出会っている。当時、フィッツジェラルドの方が有名だったのだが、フィッツジェラルドは一目でヘミングウェイの才能を見抜き、彼を出版社に売り込んだり、彼の小説にアドバイスをした。その後、フィッツジェラルドよりヘミングウェイの方が有名になったのだが、二人の友情は生涯にわたって続いたという。ちなみに、村上春樹が挙げる最も影響を受けた3冊の本のなかには、フィッツジェラルドの『グレート・ギャッツビー』が入っている。

Keywords

本文に使われている次の語句の意味としてもっとも適切なものを a～h から選びなさい。

1.	(l.2) take place	a. 10 年間	1. (	)
2.	(l.10) immediately	b. を認める、～が分かる	2. (	)
3.	(l.10) recognize	c. 行われる、起きる	3. (	)
4.	(l.17) whereas	d. 突然の、急な	4. (	)
5.	(l.17) decade	e. …だが一方、しかるに…	5. (	)
6.	(l.22) sudden	f. ～にもかかわらず	6. (	)
7.	(blank) in contrast	g. 対照的に、逆に	7. (	)
8.	(blank) despite	h. すぐに、ただちに	8. (	)

Unit 5 Literature

   In April 1925, two great American writers of the twentieth century met each other for the first time. The meeting took place in France, not the United States—at the Dingo Bar in Paris. Those two writers were F. Scott Fitzgerald and Ernest Hemingway.

   At the time of their meeting, F. Scott Fitzgerald was already a famous writer. He had just completed his novel *The Great Gatsby*, which marked the high point of his career. (A), Hemingway was not well known. He had written some short stories, but most appeared in small magazines that only a few people read.

   Fitzgerald immediately recognized Hemingway's talent and tried to help him by recommending him to the large publishing company Scribner's. Fitzgerald also gave Hemingway good advice on how to improve the novel he was writing. That novel, titled *The Sun Also Rises*, was published by Scribner's in 1926.

   (B), Hemingway became famous—and soon he became more popular among readers than Fitzgerald was. In the 1930s, Hemingway wrote several best-selling books; whereas Fitzgerald's popularity was falling. That decade was also a difficult time for Fitzgerald's personal life. Hemingway did not do much to help his old friend, however. One reason for his unkindness might have been that Hemingway was busy dealing with his own personal problems.

   (C), Fitzgerald kept on writing until his death of a heart attack in 1940, at the age of 44. Because of his sudden death he was unable to finish a novel about Hollywood that he was writing. After his death, more and more readers became interested in his writing, and soon he was more popular than he had ever been while living.

   Hemingway also kept writing until his death, which came in 1961. But the final years were difficult ones. It became harder and harder for him to write as his health got worse. But in his last years Hemingway wrote about his early years in Paris and his friendship with Fitzgerald. Even though he had been unkind to Fitzgerald at times, that friendship was very important to Hemingway.

(351 words)

Friends and Rivals

Exercises

1 本文中の空欄（ A ），（ B ），（ C ）に入る語句として最も適切なものを下の①～③の中から選びなさい。

(A) _____
(B) _____
(C) _____

> ① In contrast
> ② Despite his loss of popularity
> ③ Thanks to that novel

2 本文全体のトピックセンテンス（主題文）を探して、該当する英文に下線を引きなさい。

3 質問を読み、正しい答を (A) ～ (D) の中から選びなさい。

Question 1

What is the main topic of this passage?

(A) American literature in the twentieth century
(B) The relationship between two American writers
(C) An analysis of the writing of Hemingway and Fitzgerald
(D) The many writers who lived in Paris in the 1920s and 1930s

Question 2

What is true about Hemingway in 1925?

(A) He was less famous than Fitzgerald was.
(B) He was at the high point of his career.
(C) He tried to help his good friend Fitzgerald.
(D) He always did his writing at the Dingo Bar.

Unit 5 Literature

4 次の英文は本文の内容に関するものである。本文の内容に一致する場合はTを、一致しない場合はFを下線部に記入しなさい。

(a) Hemingway was as popular as Fitzgerald in the 1930s.
_____

(b) Fitzgerald was able to continue writing thanks to Hemingway's help.
_____

(c) Fitzgerald became more popular after his death than when he had been living.
_____

5 a. に続く b. c. d. の英文を正しく並べ替えて本文の要約文を完成させ、正しい順序を下線部に記入しなさい。また、空欄（ A),(B),(C),(D) に入れるべき人名として、① Fitzgerald か、② Hemingway を選びなさい。

a. Two of the greatest American writers of the twentieth century, F. Scott Fitzgerald and Ernest Hemingway, were friends.
_____

b. They met in 1926, at the time when (A) was famous but (B) was not well known.

c. Soon (C) became more famous than (D).

d. Fitzgerald helped his friend in many ways.
_____

e. Hemingway did not do much to help his friend when he needed help in the 1930s, but after Fitzgerald's death he looked back on his friendship with good memories.

正しい順序   a → _____ → _____ → _____ → e

(A) _____ (B) _____ (C) _____ (D) _____

① Fitzgerald
② Hemingway

6 空欄に適切な単語を書き入れて英訳文を完成させなさい。アルファベットが与えられている場合はその文字で始めること。

(a) 市場シェアを獲得するために、商売上のライバルはしばしば互いに相手より安い価格で商品を売る。

Business rivals often offer goods (　　　) lower prices than (　　　) other in order to win market share.

(b) 必要不可欠な部品がないため、私たちは試作品を完成させることができない。

We can't (c　　　　) the prototype as we are missing an (es　　　　) component.

(c) 強力な証拠があるにもかかわらず、彼の助言を誰も聞き入れなかったことには、彼自身が驚いた。

He himself was surprised that no one listened to his suggestion (de　　　　) the strong (e　　　　).

(d) いかなる急な動作によって生じる所有物の破損・紛失に対しても、電鉄会社は責任を負わない。

The train company is not liable for damaged or lost property (c　　　　) by any (s　　　　) motion.

(e) 新型モデルのほうがかっこよく見える一方で、価格面では旧モデルのほうが優れていた。

The new model (s　　　　) more stylish (wh　　　　) the old model has a better price.

Unit 6　Tourism

中国からの旅行者

Chinese Overseas

中国人が日本で行う「爆買い(shopping spree)」についてしばしば報道されるが、実際、中国人はアジアを中心に世界中に旅行し、彼らが使うお金はアメリカ人旅行者が使うお金よりも多くなっている。このため、ホテル、レストランや小売店は中国語で応対できるスタッフを置くのが当たり前になってきており、案内やメニューは中国語のものを揃えている。海外旅行者は文化的な違いが原因でトラブルを起こすこともあるが、旅行者の落とすお金は、多くの国で歓迎されていることも事実である。

Keywords

本文に使われている次の語句の意味としてもっとも適切なものを a～h から選びなさい。

1.	(l.2) benefit from	a. 常に大量に金を使う人	1. ( )
2.	(l.4) spender	b. ～から利益を得る	2. ( )
3.	(l.5) billion	c. ～（する）と予想される	3. ( )
4.	(l.7) be expected to *do*	d. 手頃な（値段の）、無理なく買える	4. ( )
5.	(l.18) back home	e. 個人の、個別の	5. ( )
6.	(l.21) individual	f. 10億の	6. ( )
7.	(l.27) affordable	g. 時々	7. ( )
8.	(l.28) at times	h. 祖国の；祖国では	8. ( )

In recent years, the number of Chinese tourists traveling to foreign countries has increased rapidly. Many countries are benefiting from the spending of Chinese tourists. In fact, in 2012, the Chinese became the biggest tourist spenders on overseas trips. That year 83 million Chinese traveled overseas, spending a total of 102 billion US dollars, which is more than the amount of money that American tourists spent. The number of Chinese tourists traveling overseas is expected to increase soon to 100 million.

Hotels, restaurants, and stores in major tourist destinations are trying to make changes to attract more Chinese tourists. It is common now for major hotels and shopping centers in many countries to have staff who can speak Chinese, (A) restaurants are also introducing Chinese-language menus.

Many Chinese who are traveling overseas for the first time prefer to go on "package tours." This makes it easy for them to travel because all of the decisions on hotels, restaurants, and tourist sites are decided by the company organizing the tour. The Chinese that travel on package tours often visit several cities or countries in just a few days. The important thing for them is to be able to take some photographs of famous places and buy presents for friends back home.

(B) Chinese with more travel experience often prefer to organize their own trip, rather than relying on a package tour. Young people, in particular, prefer this individual approach. Such tourists feel comfortable traveling abroad because they often have good language skills and have met many foreigners through their university studies or jobs.

(C) more and more Chinese are traveling to Europe, Asia remains the main destination for Chinese tourists. The most popular country for Chinese tourists is Thailand, followed by Hong Kong and Macao. Thailand is popular because it is located near China, affordable, and full of friendly people.

At times, the arrival of huge numbers of Chinese tourists can create problems because of cultural differences. But most countries welcome these tourists as a great business opportunity.

(337 words)

Unit 6 Tourism

Exercises

1 本文中の空欄（ A),（ B),（ C ）に入る語句として最も適切なものを下の①～③の中から選びなさい。なお、文頭に来る文字も小文字で表している。

(A) _____
(B) _____
(C) _____

> ① although
> ② but
> ③ and

2 本文全体のトピックセンテンス（主題文）を探して、該当する英文に下線を引きなさい。

3 質問を読み、正しい答を (A) ～ (D) の中から選びなさい。

Question 1

Which of the following sentences best describes the main topic of this article?

(A) Younger Chinese tourists do not like package tours.
(B) China has been making a lot of money from tourism.
(C) Chinese tourism has been causing problems overseas.
(D) More and more Chinese are traveling to foreign countries.

Question 2

What happened in 2012?

(A) More than 83 million tourists traveled to China that year.
(B) American tourists spent a total of 102 billion US dollars in China.
(C) Chinese tourists spent more money overseas than American tourists.
(D) The number of Chinese tourists traveling overseas increased to 100 million.

4 次の英文は本文の内容に関するものである。本文の内容に一致する場合は T を、一致しない場合は F を下線部に記入しなさい。

(a) It has become common for Chinese hotels and shopping centers to open overseas.
_____

(b) Inexperienced Chinese tourists tend to prefer package tours.
_____

(c) Europe has become the most popular tourist destination for Chinese.
_____

5 a. に続く b. c. d. の英文を正しく並べ替えて本文の要約文を完成させ、正しい順序を下線部に記入しなさい。また、空欄（ A),（ B),（ C ）に入る最も適切な語句を①〜③の中から選びなさい。

a. The number of Chinese tourists taking overseas trips has been increasing in recent years.
_____

b. Now, hotels, restaurants, and shops are trying to (A) Chinese tourists.

c. In 2012, Chinese spent the most money as tourists—over 100 billion US dollars.

d. As the tourists (B) more experienced travelers, they are preferring to (C) their own trips, rather than traveling on package tours.

正しい順序　a → _____ → _____ → _____

(A) _____　(B) _____　(C) _____

① attract
② organize
③ become

Unit 6 Tourism

6 空欄に適切な単語を書き入れて英訳文を完成させなさい。アルファベットが与えられている場合はその文字で始めること。

(a) そのプロジェクトは、金曜日までに終了する予定だった。

The project (   ) (e   ) to be finished by Friday.

(b) その海岸といくつかの離れ島は、人気のある観光目的地である。

The coast and outlying islands are (p   ) tourist (d   ).

(c) インターネット経由の電話がますます一般化してきている。

Making telephone calls via the Internet is (b   ) more and more (c   ).

(d) あなたのレポートをもっと明確にするために、私は少し調整を加えた。

I made some adjustments to your report in order to (m   ) (   ) more clear.

(e) 物価が上昇しているので、一つの収入のみに頼るのは危険かもしれない。

With costs rising, (r   ) solely (   ) one salary might be risky.

Unit 7 Social Problems

スマホ依存症

Loving Your Smartphone (Too Much)

スマートフォンを常に触っていないと気が済まなかったり、不安になったりする人が増えているが、これを「スマホ依存症」と言う。スマホを忘れると不安になったり、大した用もないのに常にスマホを触っている、また、友だち・家族などといても、いつもスマホを触っている、歩いているときでも、食事中でもスマホを触っている…、などなど。最近では使用したアプリを監視して、どのアプリに多くの時間を使っているのかを知らせるアプリまで登場している。

Keywords

本文に使われている次の語句の意味としてもっとも適切なものを a～j から選びなさい。

1. (l.1) be addicted to	a. 返信、返事	1. (　　)
2. (l.2) psychologist	b. 携帯電話依存症	2. (　　)
3. (l.8) have access to	c. アプリ	3. (　　)
4. (l.13) miss out	d. 心理学者	4. (　　)
5. (l.14) nomophobia	e. ～を利用できる	5. (　　)
6. (l.22) notify	f. ～に言及する	6. (　　)
7. (l.23) response	g. 機会を逃す	7. (　　)
8. (l.24) app	h. ～の中毒になっている	8. (　　)
9. (l.25) monitor	i. ～を監視する	9. (　　)
10. (blank) refer to	j. ～に知らせる	10. (　　)

Unit 7 Social Problems

　　Is it possible to be "addicted" to a smartphone just like some people are addicted to cigarettes or to alcohol? Some psychologists believe that it is possible for a person to become dependent on a smartphone.

　　Especially for young people, smartphones have become the most important way to (A) other people. This is one reason why many people are constantly using their smartphone to check their email or social networking services like Facebook or Twitter. Research has shown that heavy users of smartphones become very nervous if they do not have access to their smartphones, even for a short period of time. This research suggests that there are people who are psychologically dependent on their smartphones.

　　Some new terms have even been created to (B) the fear that people have of not having access to their phones. One term is FOMO—or the "fear of missing out." This is the feeling that if you do not check your smartphone you will miss some important opportunity. A different term is "nomophobia"—or "no-mobile-phone-phobia." This is the feeling of stress that some people have if they are not able to use their smartphone for a certain period of time.

　　Smartphones have become important not only as a way to stay connected to friends, but also as a tool for thinking. People rely on Internet searches to find important information. This is one reason why people feel nervous if they do not have access to their smartphone.

　　So what can be done if a person becomes addicted to a smartphone? One simple idea is to (C) the function that notifies you when you have received a new email or a response on Twitter or Facebook.

　　But some people are actually buying new apps to help them use their smartphone less often. Such apps monitor your smartphone use and tell you what apps you are spending the most time on. This makes it clear when your smartphone use has increased too much.

(332 words)

Loving Your Smartphone (Too Much)

Exercises

1 本文中の空欄（ A ），（ B ），（ C ）に入る語句として最も適切なものを下の①〜③の中から選びなさい。なお、文頭に来る文字も小文字で表している。

(A) _____
(B) _____
(C) _____

① turn off
② refer to
③ stay connected to

2 本文全体のトピックセンテンス（主題文）を探して、該当する英文に下線を引きなさい。

3 質問を読み、正しい答を (A) 〜 (D) の中から選びなさい。

Question 1

What is the main topic of this article?

(A) Addictions to cigarettes, alcohol, and smartphones
(B) The problem of being dependent on a smartphone
(C) New apps that make smartphones more convenient
(D) The general problem of addiction that some people have

Question 2

What is "nomophobia"?

(A) A fear of missing out on using a smartphone
(B) A new term that has the same meaning as FOMO
(C) A negative feeling caused by not being able to use a smartphone
(D) Stress that comes from using a smartphone over a certain period of time

Unit 7　Social Problems

4 次の英文は本文の内容に関するものである。本文の内容に一致する場合はTを、一致しない場合はFを下線部に記入しなさい。

(a) Psychologists all believe that smartphones are addictive.
　_____

(b) Research suggests that people are dependent on Facebook and Twitter.
　_____

(c) There are new apps designed to help people use smartphones less.
　_____

5 a. に続く b. c. d. の英文を正しく並べ替えて本文の要約文を完成させ、正しい順序を下線部に記入しなさい。また、空欄（ A),(B),(C) に入る最も適切な語句を①〜③の中から選びなさい。

a. Smartphones are very convenient devices, (A) some people are using them too often.
_____

b. Some psychologists even think (B) it is possible to be addicted to a smartphone, much like being addicted to cigarettes or alcohol.

c. New smartphone apps have been developed to help people reduce the time they spend on their smartphones.

d. Heavy users of smartphones often feel nervous or stressed (C) they cannot access their device.

正しい順序　a → _____ → _____ → _____

(A) _____　(B) _____　(C) _____

① but
② if
③ that

Loving Your Smartphone (Too Much)

6 空欄に適切な単語を書き入れて英訳文を完成させなさい。アルファベットが与えられている場合はその文字で始めること。

(a) 集中しつづけることが、目標達成に重要である。

(S) focused is important in order to (a) one's objectives.

(b) その病院は、医療研究に対し、実践的で現場志向のアプローチを重視している。

The hospital emphasizes a (p), reality-oriented approach to medical (r).

(c) チャールズは終電に乗り遅れないように即座にオフィスを出た。

Charles (l) his office quickly so as not to (m) the last train.

(d) 急成長の市場により、事業を始める新たな機会が数多く創出された。

The fast-growing market (c) many new (o) for starting businesses.

(e) 発送が遅れることを、当社の顧客に知らせてください。

Please (n) our client that the shipment will be (d).

Unit 8 Sociology

高齢社会と向き合う

Dealing with the Graying Population

世界中の多くの国で 65 歳以上の人口の割合が伸びている。こうした国では老齢化に伴って数多くの問題に直面しており、日本も例外ではない。現在、日本の 65 歳以上の人口の割合は約 25% であり、世界で一番高い。さらに、問題は老齢化の先にある人口減少だ。2015 年に 1 億 2 千 7 百万人あった人口が、2050 年には 1 億人を下回るという。こうした問題は年金問題にも大きな影響を及ぼす。解決策はあるのだろうか？

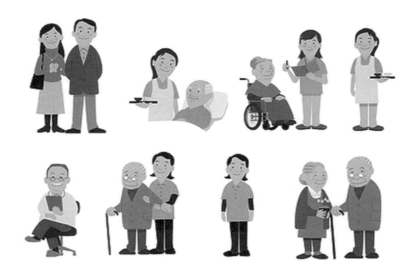

Keywords

本文に使われている次の語句の意味としてもっとも適切なものを a〜h から選びなさい。

1.	(l.6) be expected to *do*	a. 年金	1. ( )
2.	(l.8) proportion	b. 割合、比率	2. ( )
3.	(l.12) pension	c. 看護、介護	3. ( )
4.	(l.20) respond	d. 縮む、小さくなる	4. ( )
5.	(l.21) cope with	e. 〜すると予想 [予定] される	5. ( )
6.	(l.24) interact with	f. 〜に対処する	6. ( )
7.	(l.26) nursing care	g. 反応する、応じる；返答する	7. ( )
8.	(l.29) shrink	h. 〜と仲良くなる、ふれあう	8. ( )

Dealing with the Graying Population

In many countries around the world, the percentage of people who are 65 years or older has been increasing. These countries are facing numerous problems related to this rapidly aging population.

Japan is one of the countries facing the most significant population decrease. In 2014, the country's population was just under 127 million people, but by 2040 the population is expected to fall to around 107 million—and by 2050 the population will probably be under 100 million. Moreover, the proportion of the Japanese population that is 65 years or older is around 25% today—the highest percentage in the world. (A), that percentage was only 7% in 1970. This high percentage of elderly people, who usually are not working, has created financial problems for Japan. (B), it is becoming difficult for the country to pay for the pensions and medical care of retired people.

So what can Japan do to deal with this situation? One obvious idea that many people have proposed is to extend the "working age" in Japan. (C), people in Japan have usually stopped working around the age of 65. If people would retire at 70 instead, this would increase the working population, so that there would be more people to support the elderly and retired. Another benefit of people working longer is that by being active at work, these older workers can stay healthy and also maintain their connection to society.

As the population gets older in Japan, companies are responding by creating products for elderly consumers. Some products may help Japan cope with its aging population. One example is the development of robot pets. More and more elderly people are lonely because they are living alone. But taking care of a real pet can be difficult for them. Interacting with a robot pet is one way for elderly people to feel less lonely. There are also robots that can assist with nursing care. Robot suits are also being developed that make it easier for a person to move or lift heavy objects.

Japan will need such technologies, as well as policy changes, if it hopes to respond successfully to its shrinking population.

(362 words)

Unit 8   Sociology

Exercises

1 本文中の空欄（ A),（ B),（ C) に入る語句として最も適切なものを下の①〜③の中から選びなさい。

(A) _____
(B) _____
(C) _____

> ① Up to now
> ② In particular
> ③ In contrast

2 本文全体のトピックセンテンス（主題文）を探して、該当する英文に下線を引きなさい。

3 質問を読み、正しい答を (A)〜(D) の中から選びなさい。

Question 1

What is one of the main topics of this article?

(A) Ideas for increasing Japan's population quickly
(B) Some ways for Japan to deal with its population problem
(C) The ways technology has solved Japan's population problem
(D) Economic growth resulting from Japan's decreasing population

Question 2

What is expected to happen in the future in Japan?

(A) Around 25% will be 65 or older in a few years.
(B) Only 7% of the working population will be elderly.
(C) The population will fall to under 127 million by 2040.
(D) Population will be below 100 million by 2050.

4

次の英文は本文の内容に関するものである。本文の内容に一致する場合は T を、一致しない場合は F を下線部に記入しなさい。

(a) Many Japanese volunteered to retire at 70 instead of 65.
　_____

(b) Robot pets have been developed for older consumers.
　_____

(c) Robots are the only solution to Japan's population problem.
　_____

5

a. に続く b. c. d. の英文を正しく並べ替えて本文の要約文を完成させ、正しい順序を下線部に記入しなさい。また、空欄 (A), (B), (C) に入る最も適切な語句を①～③の中から選びなさい。

a. Japan's population has been decreasing steadily.

b. This large number of elderly people is creating (A) for the country.

c. Already, the country has a higher percentage of people 65 or older than any other country.

d. Japan will need to come up with (B), such as extending the working age or introducing (C).

正しい順序　a → _____ → _____ → _____

(A) _____　(B) _____　(C) _____

> ① new technologies
> ② financial problems
> ③ solutions

Unit 8　Sociology

6 空欄に適切な単語を書き入れて英訳文を完成させなさい。アルファベットが与えられている場合はその文字で始めること。

(a) そのビルの完成は来年3月初旬と予想されている。

The completion of the building (　　　) (e　　　　) to be early next March.

(b) その新しい年金制度は、若い人たちにあまりよく受け入れられなかった。

The new (　　　　) system was not (r　　　　) well by young people.

(c) 顧客からの不満に迅速に対応することは、顧客サービスの重要な要素である。

Being prompt in (r　　　　) (t　　) customer complaints is an important part of customer service.

(d) 隣家の吠える犬をうまくあしらうのには苦労している。

I'm having (d　　　　) (c　　　　) with my neighbor's barking dogs.

(e) 会社の利益が減ってきているので、従業員への賞与は減らされるだろう。

As company (p　　　　) have (s　　　　), employee bonuses will have to be cut.

Unit 9 Animals

金色の毒ガエル

Golden Poison Frog

Golden poison frog はコロンビアに生息するカエルで、体色はオレンジ色、黄色、薄緑色などに変化する。小さな色鮮やかなカエルだが、その名のとおり毒を持っており、コロンビアの原住民はこのカエルから毒を抽出して、矢に塗って狩りをした。このカエルの毒は猛毒で、わずか1ミリグラムの毒で1万匹のネズミを殺せると言われている。現在は絶滅危惧種に指定されている。

Keywords

本文に使われている次の語句の意味としてもっとも適切なものをa~kから選びなさい。

1. (l.4) poison
2. (l.5) derive from
3. (l.5) outstanding
4. (l.5) trait
5. (l.12) potency
6. (l.15) in ... terms
7. (l.16) lethal [líːθəl]
8. (l.17) be heralded as
9. (l.24) clothe
10. (l.28) hence
11. (blank) dazzling

a. 特徴、特色
b. 効力、効能
c. 毒、毒物
d. ～に衣服を与える
e. ～として（一般に）告げ知らされる
f. ～に由来する
g. 死を招く、致命的な
h. 顕著な；優れた
i. まばゆい、きらきらする
j. ～の観点で
k. それゆえ、だから

1. (　)
2. (　)
3. (　)
4. (　)
5. (　)
6. (　)
7. (　)
8. (　)
9. (　)
10. (　)
11. (　)

Unit 9 Animals

The most dangerous animal in the world is not a lion nor a tiger nor even a poisonous snake. That title instead belongs to a small, brightly colored frog living in the Pacific jungles of Colombia in South America—a frog named the "golden poison frog".

The name derives from the frog's two outstanding traits. While sometimes green or orange, the frog is often a very rich yellow in color. This yellow can sometimes seem (A) gold. The skin of the frog is then coated with a thin layer of poison. This coating of poison is only for self-defense, as the frog will never attack other animals. Yet, to touch the frog will bring certain death. The golden yellow almost serves as a warning for other creatures to back off and stay away.

How deadly is the golden poison frog? The potency varies from frog to frog, but scientists estimate the average golden poison frog carries about one milligram of a poison so powerful that a single frog could kill 10,000 mice. In human terms, one milligram of this poison might kill (B) twenty adults and, if a full gram, the poison might be lethal enough to take the lives of 15,000 people. The frog might thus be heralded as the most dangerous animal on earth.

The golden poison frog is small, at most only five centimeters in length. Yet, it has had a large impact on the traditional cultures of the Colombian rainforest. People there learned about the poison long ago and have applied it to their hunting. They dip darts into the frog poison and use these darts to shoot and kill larger animals, which they then skin or cook for food. Thus, for centuries, the little golden poison frog has helped feed and clothe the native peoples of the Colombian jungles.

Pretty to see, but impossible to touch, the golden poison frog presents no danger to anyone (C) it is left alone. The world's most dangerous animal hence lives a tranquil and colorful life deep in the jungles of Colombia.

(349 words)

Exercises

1 本文中の空欄（ A ），（ B ），（ C ）に入る語句として最も適切なものを下の①〜③の中から選びなさい。

(A) _____

(B) _____

(C) _____

> ① as many as
> ② as dazzling as
> ③ as long as

2 本文全体のトピックセンテンス（主題文）を探して、該当する英文に下線を引きなさい。

3 質問を読み、正しい答を (A) 〜 (D) の中から選びなさい。

Question 1

Which sentence best shows the central idea of this passage?

(A) The golden poison frog is a major threat to human life.

(B) The golden poison frog is not dangerous if left alone.

(C) The golden poison frog is dangerous, but only to mice.

(D) People have long used the golden poison frog for hunting.

Question 2

Typically how poisonous is one golden poison frog?

(A) Poisonous enough to kill lions and tigers

(B) Poisonous enough to kill twenty people

(C) Poisonous enough to kill 15,000 human beings

(D) Not poisonous at all unless it is touched

Unit 9　Animals

4 次の英文は本文の内容に関するものである。本文の内容に一致する場合はTを、一致しない場合はFを下線部に記入しなさい。

(a) The golden poison frog is always a golden yellow.
　_____

(b) The golden poison frog has had a positive impact on the human societies of the Colombian jungle.
　_____

(c) All golden poison frogs are equally poisonous.
　_____

5 a. に続く b. c. d. の英文を正しく並べ替えて本文の要約文を完成させ、正しい順序を下線部に記入しなさい。また、空欄（ A),(B),(C) に入る最も適切な語句を①〜③の中から選び、必要に応じて正しい活用形に変化させなさい。

a. The golden poison frog is a small frog living in the Pacific jungles of Colombia.

b. However, local cultures have long (A) the poison of the golden poison frog for hunting and killing larger animals for food and clothing.

c. The skin of the frog is (B) with a very deadly poison, (C) it perhaps the most dangerous animal in the world.

d. The frog does not employ this poison as weapon but as a means of self-defense.

　　正しい順序　a → _____ → _____ → _____

　(A) _____　(B) _____　(C) _____

　　① make
　　② use
　　③ coat

6 空欄に適切な単語を書き入れて英訳文を完成させなさい。アルファベットが与えられている場合はその文字で始めること。

(a) 英語の単語のほとんどは、ラテン語、フランス語、ドイツ語に由来する。

Most English words are (d   ) (   ) Latin, French and German.

(b) 子どもたちは、病気の動物を世話する上で優れた仕事をした。

The children did an (o   ) job in looking (   ) the sick animals.

(c) 裁判官はこの処罰が他の者への警告に役立つだろうと言った。

The judge said the punishment would (s   ) as a (   ) to others.

(d) ホテルのスイートルームは、町のどこにそのホテルがあるかによって料金が異なる。

Hotel suites (v   ) in price depending (   ) what part of town the hotel is in.

(e) 6か月以上購読される方には、割引購読価格が適用されます。

A reduced subscription (r   ) (a   ) if you subscribe for more than six months.

Unit 10 Art

シェイカー教徒の手づくり家具

Shaker Furniture

> Shakerは18世紀イギリスで始まったプロテスタントの一派で、その後、アメリカに移住した。シェーカー教徒は質素・誠実・公正を教理とした自給自足の共同生活を行い、一時は6,000人ぐらいまで増えたが、20世紀にはかなりのマイノリティーになった。このように非常に小規模な一派だったのだが、現在でも彼らが生活の中で作った家具は、簡素で機能的美しさを備えた巧芸品として高い評価を得ており、ニューヨークのメトロポリタン美術館をはじめ、多くの美術館で展示されている。

Keywords

本文に使われている次の語句の意味としてもっとも適切なものをa~lから選びなさい。

1. (l.1) principle	a. 実用性、効用；公共事業	1. ( )
2. (l.2) simplicity	b. 思い出させるもの［人］	2. ( )
3. (l.6) house	c. 質素；単純；簡単	3. ( )
4. (l.11) stain	d. 主義；原理、原則	4. ( )
5. (l.11) critical	e. ～することに意欲的である	5. ( )
6. (l.12) utility	f. を保管する、を格納する	6. ( )
7. (l.13) on occasion	g. を着色する、を染色する	7. ( )
8. (l.13) with precision	h. 骨董品の	8. ( )
9. (l.17) plentiful	i. たくさんの、豊富な	9. ( )
10. (l.18) be willing to *do*	j. 重要な；批判的な；重篤な	10. ( )
11. (l.26) antique	k. 正確に、緻密に	11. ( )
12. (l.29) reminder	l. 時々	12. ( )

Shaker Furniture

The "Shakers" is the nickname of a Christian group known for its principles of simplicity and honesty. Founded in England in the 18th century, the group later settled in the United States and, while still active today, currently has far fewer members than it once did. (A) the Shakers will not long be forgotten due to their contribution to American art. What was their art form, a form considered so dynamic and clean that it is now housed in museums across the land? Furniture! The Shakers became famous for creating beautiful furniture.

Just as simplicity was a central idea to their Christian lifestyle, simplicity was also key to the success of Shaker's furniture. The chairs, cabinets, dressers and tables have straight lines with no added decorations. While the furniture was sometimes stained with various colors, the critical feature was not beauty but utility. However, Shaker furniture is indeed beautiful. (B) the Shakers used nails on occasion, in most cases they fit pieces together with careful precision, using only wood and glue. The appeal of Shaker furniture lies in the natural attractiveness of the wood.

For the Shakers, making such furniture became more than a matter of personal need. They had plentiful furniture for their own communities, but soon found outside people were more than willing to purchase high-quality Shaker chairs and cabinets. Thus, furniture-making became a steady means of income for the Shakers. (C) the modern world has turned more and more to mass-produced goods, Shaker furniture has become a symbol for the better product of the skilled individual craftsman.

Today many museums are proud to display Shaker furniture, with the most visited such display being in the Metropolitan Museum of Art in New York City. Shaker furniture is also collected by private individuals, just as some people collect fine paintings and sculpture. Antique Shaker furniture in good condition can sell for hundreds if not thousands of dollars.

Nowadays the Shakers are mostly gone, but their furniture is not. It continues as a reminder of the simple and clean lifestyle of the Shaker communities.

(344 words)

Unit 10 Art

Exercises

1 本文中の空欄（ A ），(B ），(C ）に入る語句として最も適切なものを下の①～③の中から選びなさい。

(A) _____
(B) _____
(C) _____

> ① Although
> ② As
> ③ Yet

2 本文全体のトピックセンテンス（主題文）を探して、該当する英文に下線を引きなさい。

3 質問を読み、正しい答を (A) ～ (D) の中から選びなさい。

Question 1

Which sentence best sums up the key idea of this passage?

(A) The Shakers produced furniture that is now kept only in museums.
(B) Although living a simple lifestyle, the Shakers were able to profit from selling furniture.
(C) The Shakers' simple lifestyle is reflected in the beauty of their handmade furniture.
(D) These days, antique Shaker furniture can be very expensive.

Question 2

What is a central feature of Shaker furniture?

(A) Mass production for increased profit
(B) Wood with decorative markings
(C) A reliance on the natural beauty of wood
(D) The consistent use of nails

Shaker Furniture

4 次の英文は本文の内容に関するものである。本文の内容に一致する場合はTを、一致しない場合はFを下線部に記入しなさい。

(a) Shaker furniture is no longer bought and sold.
_____

(b) The Shakers no longer exist.
_____

(c) The Shakers originated outside the United States.
_____

5 a. に続く b. c. d. の英文を正しく並べ替えて本文の要約文を完成させ、正しい順序を下線部に記入しなさい。また、空欄（ A),(B),(C) に入る最も適切な語句を①〜③の中から選びなさい。

a. The Shakers are a Christian group that (A) based on principles of simplicity and honesty.

b. Shaker furniture (B) for its simple design and beautiful wood.

c. Today many examples of Shaker furniture are kept in museums and antique Shaker furniture can be very expensive.

d. These beliefs (C) the Shakers made furniture.

e. The Shakers thus had a large impact on American art.

正しい順序　a → _____ → _____ → _____ → e

(A) _____　(B) _____　(C) _____

① became renowned
② formed communities
③ influenced the way

Unit 10　Art

6 空欄に適切な単語を書き入れて英訳文を完成させなさい。アルファベットが与えられている場合はその文字で始めること。

(a) 計画の簡潔さが、その最大の長所である。

The (s   ) of the plan is its (   ) point.

(b) 1636年に創立されて、ハーヴァード大学はアメリカ合衆国で最も古い大学である。

(F   ) ( ) the year 1636, Harvard is the oldest university in the United States.

(c) 会社は、私たちの力が及ばない状況になったために破産した。

Our company went bankrupt (d) to circumstances that were (b   ) our control.

(d) カレンダーの丸印を見ると、いつも締め切りを思い出す。

The circle on the calendar is a constant (r   ) ( ) the deadline.

(e) 機関投資家は、個人よりもリスクの高い事業に投資できる立場にある。

Institutions are in a position to invest in riskier ventures (   ) (i   ) are.

Unit 11 Food

夢の食品、チア・シード

Chia Seeds—the Super Food

> Chia [tʃíːə] seed は中南部メキシコとガテマラを原産とするミント植物 chia の種であるが、現在ではその豊富な栄養素（ビタミン B1, B2, B3、タンパク質、カルシウムなど）が健康に良いと欧米や日本でサプリメントとして人気がある。Chia seed はまた、ほとんどカロリーがなく、においもないので、いろいろな食品に加えて摂取しやすく、繊維も豊富に含むのでダイエット効果も大きい。

Keywords

本文に使われている次の語句の意味としてもっとも適切なものを a〜l から選びなさい。

1. (l.1) glance	a. 栄養素、栄養物	1. ( )
2. (l.9) healthful	b. 肥満	2. ( )
3. (l.12) plentiful	c. 繊維	3. ( )
4. (l.12) nutrient	d. たんぱく質	4. ( )
5. (l.13) protein	e. 一瞥、ちら見	5. ( )
6. (l.15) fiber	f. 〜に溶け込む、混ざる	6. ( )
7. (l.20) nutritional	g. 前代未聞の、前例のない	7. ( )
8. (l.21) fit	h. 健康に良い	8. ( )
9. (l.22) obesity	i. 奇跡的な、すばらしい	9. ( )
10. (l.22) unheard-of	j. 栄養の、栄養のある	10. ( )
11. (l.22) miraculous	k. 豊富な、たくさんの	11. ( )
12. (l.26) blend	l. 健康な、元気な	12. ( )

Unit 11 Food

At a glance the tiny seeds of the chia plant do not seem very special. They tend to be black or gray in color and are less than a tenth the size of a grain of rice. Chew them and they have almost no flavor. Yet, these small seeds are now gaining worldwide attention as a new "super food," one that can help provide modern man with a healthier and happier diet.

Chia plants grow naturally in both Central America and Mexico. The plant itself is a member of the mint family and the seeds have been used as an important food source for hundreds of years, dating back to before the days of Columbus. They have continued to be a healthful addition to the Central and South American diet even up to present times. Yet, these days the value of chia seeds is becoming known to the world at large.

What makes chia seeds so super? To start, they contain plentiful nutrients, such as protein and calcium and vitamins such as B1, B2 and B3. But (A) this chia seeds have almost no calories. They add nutrients without adding weight. Chia seeds are also forty percent fiber, making them one of the finest fiber sources in the world.

(B) the high amount of fiber, chia seeds can absorb over ten times their weight in liquid and therefore will expand once inside the stomach. This can help people feel naturally full and prevent them from overeating. Chia seeds thus are not only good for the diet (C) nutritional content but they can also help people stay slim and fit. As advanced societies struggle with issues of obesity, chia seeds offer an unheard-of, almost miraculous solution, that of allowing people to avoid unnecessary weight through the simple and enjoyable act of eating.

In our fat-conscious, health-sensitive world, chia seeds are now finding increased popularity. They have no special flavor and thus blend easily into other dishes. They match any meal—breakfast, lunch or dinner. They are a super food indeed.

(347 words)

Chia Seeds—the Super Food

Exercises

1 本文中の空欄（ A ），（ B ），（ C ）に入る語句として最も適切なものを下の①〜③の中から選びなさい。なお、文頭に来る文字も小文字で表している。

(A) _____
(B) _____
(C) _____

> ① due to
> ② in the sense of
> ③ on top of

2 本文全体のトピックセンテンス（主題文）を探して、該当する英文に下線を引きなさい。

3 質問を読み、正しい答を (A) 〜 (D) の中から選びなさい。

Question 1

Why are chia seeds considered a super food?

(A) They have been an important food source for hundreds of years.

(B) They are very small, but have worldwide attention.

(C) They have high calories despite having a large amount of fiber.

(D) They are high in nutrients and fiber and can help with weight management.

Question 2

How might chia seeds help people lose weight?

(A) Chia seeds have no flavor and can mix with any kind of meal.

(B) Chia seeds can make people feel full and they will thus eat less.

(C) Chia seeds are packed with vitamins and nutrients.

(D) Chia seeds can contribute to overeating.

Unit 11　Food

4 次の英文は本文の内容に関するものである。本文の内容に一致する場合はTを、一致しない場合はFを下線部に記入しなさい。

(a) Chia seeds are a recent discovery.
　_____

(b) Chia seeds give a special taste to whatever dish they are added.
　_____

(c) Chia seeds are rich in fiber.
　_____

5 a. に続くb. c. d. の英文を正しく並べ替えて本文の要約文を完成させ、正しい順序を下線部に記入しなさい。また、空欄（ A),(B),(C ）に入る最も適切な語句を①〜③の中から選びなさい。

a. Chia seeds have been an important part of the food life of Central and South America for hundreds of years, but now are gaining international attention as a super food.
_____

b. More importantly, the high (A) might help people diet naturally.

c. That chia seeds mix well with all kinds of food is another added plus.

d. The seeds are high in (B) and low in (C).

正しい順序　a → _____ → _____ → _____

(A) _____　(B) _____　(C) _____

① calories
② nutrients
③ fiber content

Chia Seeds—the Super Food

6 空欄に適切な単語を書き入れて英訳文を完成させなさい。アルファベットが与えられている場合はその文字で始めること。

(a) 石油が豊富な資源と考えられた時代は 20 年前に終焉した。

The era when oil could be considered to be a (p   ) (r   ) was over two decades ago.

(b) 栄養食品を食べることは、健康維持のために重要である。

Eating (n   ) foods is important in order to stay (   ).

(c) わが社は実際に健康に良い食習慣をもたらす食品ガイドを作成した。

We created a food guide that actually reflects (h   ) eating (   ).

(d) わが社の第一の目標は、お客様に高品質の製品を提供することである。

The primary goal of our company is to (p   ) high-quality products (   ) customers.

(e) 私の家族の歴史は、1600 年代初頭までさかのぼる。

My family history (d   ) (   ) to the early 1600s.

Unit 12　Science/Technology

Drones

ドローンの平和的利用法

> ドローンとは元々、英語で「雄のハチ」を意味する語であるが、最近では、転じて「無人機」や「無人車両」などの無線操縦機全般を指すことがある。その用途は、初め飛行爆弾として始まったように、軍事目的の特殊な兵器として使用されたが、最近では日常生活における警備活動や消火作業、設備の保守作業などにも使用されるようになっている。Amazon.com は近い将来に配達業務に利用する計画を進めている。

Keywords

本文に使われている次の語句の意味としてもっとも適切なものを a～j から選びなさい。

1.	(l.1)	unmanned	a. 栄養剤	1. (	)
2.	(l.2)	drone	b. 殺虫剤	2. (	)
3.	(l.11)	invaluable	c. 大きな集会	3. (	)
4.	(l.12)	mountainous terrain	d. （無線操縦の）無人機	4. (	)
5.	(l.12)	blink	e. 山岳地帯	5. (	)
6.	(l.16)	intruder	f. 侵入者	6. (	)
7.	(l.18)	pesticide	g. 重大な出来事	7. (	)
8.	(l.18)	nutrient	h. 無人の	8. (	)
9.	(l.24)	rally	i. 非常に貴重な	9. (	)
10.	(l.29)	milestone	j. まばたきする	10. (	)

Because of their military applications, unmanned aerial vehicles—better known as drones—have acquired a negative image with much of the general public. This image is unfortunate because drones have numerous other usages that might prove beneficial to society.

First, drones can be very helpful in cases of natural disaster. High-flying drones can track and monitor approaching storms much better and far more safely than any manned aircraft. Once a storm strikes, drones can then tirelessly search the disaster area to seek those in need of emergency care. With earthquake, flood and tsunami relief, drones can quickly detect survivors and help rush rescue workers to the most desperate areas of need. Drones also provide invaluable help in looking for individuals lost far at sea or deep in mountainous terrains. Human eyes tire and blink, but drone eyes are always open.

Drones are also useful in various work-related fields. The most obvious of these might be in the area of security. Drones can patrol from above and can spot intruders far more efficiently than fixed cameras or watchdogs. Drones can also be used in agriculture, where they can treat fields and orchards with pesticides and nutrients in a manner far more accurate than simple spraying by hand or even by airplane. In the future, drones might even be used in construction, where they will be able to fly building materials to places that are difficult to access otherwise.

(A), the best applications for drones might be in photography. Photo-journalists can use drones to take pictures of large outdoor gatherings, such as political rallies or sporting events. Shooting pictures from above might have appeal for everyday people as well. A couple, for example, might enjoy having their outdoor wedding ceremony filmed from the air, (B) universities might one day employ drones to take shots of entrance or graduation ceremonies held outside. Photos from above might offer unique and amazing views of important milestones in life.

(C), drones are not only for the military. They can play a helpful and creative part in many areas of modern day society.

(348 words)

Unit 12 Science/Technology

Exercises

1 本文中の空欄（ A),（ B),（ C ）に入る語句として最も適切なものを下の①～③の中から選びなさい。なお、文頭に来る文字も小文字で表している。

(A) _____
(B) _____
(C) _____

① thus
② however
③ or

2 本文全体のトピックセンテンス（主題文）を探して、該当する英文に下線を引きなさい。

3 質問を読み、正しい答を (A) ～ (D) の中から選びなさい。

Question 1

What is the main idea of this text?

(A) Drones are viewed negatively by the general public.
(B) Drones are very useful in times of natural disaster.
(C) Drones have many positive uses separate from the military.
(D) Drones fly high and can see a wide area.

Question 2

According to this passage, why might a drone be more useful than a human in terms of searching for a lost person?

(A) Drones are tireless and never need a break.
(B) Drones can avoid approaching storms more efficiently.
(C) Drones are especially useful in matters of security.
(D) Drones can help with media coverage.

Drones

4 次の英文は本文の内容に関するものである。本文の内容に一致する場合はTを、一致しない場合はFを下線部に記入しなさい。

(a) In terms of security, drones are more effective than fixed cameras.
　_____

(b) Drones might have special appeal for couples at church weddings.
　_____

(c) One benefit of using drones in tracking storms is that humans need not be exposed to danger.
　_____

5 a. に続くb. c. d. の英文を正しく並べ替えて本文の要約文を完成させ、正しい順序を下線部に記入しなさい。また、空欄 (A), (B), (C) に入る最も適切な語句を①〜③の中から選びなさい。

a. Most people connect unmanned aerial vehicles with the military, but there are many other non-military uses for drones that are beneficial for (A).

b. Yet, the ability of a drone to take pictures from above might make (B) their most popular usage.

c. Many of these uses have to do with (C), either in looking for survivors of disasters or in seeking those in need of emergency care.

d. Drones can also be of benefit in fields such as security, agriculture and construction.

正しい順序　a → _____ → _____ → _____

(A) _____　(B) _____　(C) _____

① photography
② humankind
③ rescue work

Unit 12 Science/Technology

6 空欄に適切な単語を書き入れて英訳文を完成させなさい。アルファベットが与えられている場合はその文字で始めること。

(a) 自動車は、日本で最も一般的な輸送手段である。

Motor (v   ) are the most (c   ) form of transport in Japan.

(b) ジュリーは優れた写真家としての評判を得はじめていた。

Julie was beginning to (a   ) a reputation (   ) a good photographer.

(c) 一旦保証が切れたら、修理費用はすべて自分で支払わなければならない。

(O   ) the warranty has expired, you must pay all repair (   ) yourself.

(d) この工場の新しい生産システムは、他の工場にも同様に移すことができる。

The new production system in this factory can be transposed to other plants (a) (w   ).

(e) その博物館では高価な絵画を守るために、最新鋭の防犯体制が敷かれている。

The museum employs state-of-the-art (s   ) to (p   ) the precious paintings.

Unit 13 Language

Nice! 昔の意味は Not nice!

How Words Can Change

> どのような言語も時を経て変化する。英語も同じである。ただ、言葉づかいが微妙に変化したり、新しい単語が生まれるのではなく、同じ単語の意味が現在と遠い過去でまったく異なることがあるとは驚きだ。Nice! と言われたら誰でも喜ぶが、何百年も前には nice はまったく異なる意味だったという。

Keywords

本文に使われている次の語句の意味としてもっとも適切なものを a～l から選びなさい。

1.	(l.4) evolve	a. 道徳、倫理感	1. (	)
2.	(l.5) interpretation	b. 解釈；通訳	2. (	)
3.	(l.6) definition	c. 道徳、美徳	3. (	)
4.	(l.8) ignorant	d. 定義	4. (	)
5.	(l.9) hence	e. を所有する	5. (	)
6.	(l.12) ascribe A to B	f. A を B に属するとする	6. (	)
7.	(l.14) naughty	g. 進化する、発展する	7. (	)
8.	(l.14) disobedient	h. 無作法な；不適当な	8. (	)
9.	(l.14) improper	i. 言うことをきかない、無礼な	9. (	)
10.	(l.19) possess	j. わがままな；従順でない	10. (	)
11.	(l.21) morality	k. 無知の、知らない	11. (	)
12.	(l.22) virtue	l. それゆえ、だから	12. (	)

Unit 13 Language

These days, people are pleased (A) their friends consider them "nice." Yet, that was not the case hundreds of years ago, as the word "nice" had a far different meaning back then. In those days, to be called "nice" was not so very nice at all! Like life itself, language is always evolving and many words have acquired new interpretations over time.

"Nice" is a good example of how the definition of a word might change. The word "nice" can trace its roots through French back into Latin, where it carried an original meaning of "ignorant." That is also what it first meant when it entered English, around the year 1300. Hence, no one then liked to be told they were "nice." Later the meaning changed to mean "foolish" or "silly" and it was only two or three centuries ago when "nice" finally came to have the pleasant meaning we ascribe to it now.

A word that today is often thought of as the opposite of "nice" is the word "naughty." Today "naughty" can mean "disobedient" or "improper." For example, a puppy that chews house slippers might be called "naughty." (B), when "naughty" first entered the English language it simply meant "nothing." Even today some people sometimes use the word "naught" as a synonym for "zero." Thus, around 1300, "naughty people" were only those people who possessed nothing. In other words, they were poor. Soon, however, the meaning shifted to express those who had nothing of value, and this quickly evolved further and came to mean someone who lacked morality or virtue. Thus "naughty" gradually came to mean "not nice."

The well-recorded Christmas song, "Santa Claus is Coming to Town," contains a famous phrase about Santa checking to see whether children have been "naughty or nice." That's a phrase Santa could not have used in the past, (C) those words would have meant something entirely different! Instead of "good" or "bad," he would have been attempting to determine if the children were "poor" or "ignorant"!

Thus language is evolving! Who knows what "nice" and "naughty" might mean in the future?

(350 words)

How Words Can Change

Exercises

1 本文中の空欄（ A ），(B ），(C ）に入る語句として最も適切なものを下の①〜③の中から選びなさい。なお、文頭に来る文字も小文字で表している。

(A) _____
(B) _____
(C) _____

① yet
② if
③ for

2 本文全体のトピックセンテンス（主題文）を探して、該当する英文に下線を引きなさい。

3 質問を読み、正しい答を (A) 〜 (D) の中から選びなさい。

Question 1

What is the central meaning of this passage?

(A) "Naughty" used to mean "nice" and "nice" used to mean "naughty."
(B) Words can change their meanings dramatically over time.
(C) Santa Claus misuses the original meanings of "naughty" and "nice."
(D) Words have provided stability as times have changed.

Question 2

Two hundred years ago what was the likely meaning of the word, "nice"?

(A) Silly
(B) Nice
(C) Ignorant
(D) Naughty

Unit 13   Language

4   次の英文は本文の内容に関するものである。本文の内容に一致する場合はTを、一致しない場合はFを下線部に記入しなさい。

(a) A person who had no money might have been called "naughty" 1300 years ago.
_____

(b) In the song, "Santa Claus is Coming to Town," both "naughty" and "nice" have the same meanings that they do at present.
_____

(c) The meaning for "nice" evolved more slowly than the meaning for "naughty".
_____

5   a. に続くb. c. d. の英文を正しく並べ替えて本文の要約文を完成させ、正しい順序を下線部に記入しなさい。また、空欄 (A), (B), (C) に入る最も適切な語句を①〜③の中から選びなさい。

a. Words can change their meanings over time.
_____

b. In a similar way, the word "naughty" has changed meaning too.

c. The word, "nice," for example, now means someone or something that is "(A)."

d. Yet, when "nice" was first used in English, it meant "(B)" and later even "silly" or "foolish."
_____

e. It once meant "(C)" and developed its modern meanings of "disobedient" or "improper" only over time.

正しい順序   a → _____ → _____ → _____ → e

(A) _____   (B) _____   (C) _____

① nothing
② pleasant
③ ignorant

6

空欄に適切な単語を書き入れて英訳文を完成させなさい。アルファベットが与えられている場合はその文字で始めること。

(a) 教師も学生も学校の新しい体育館を気に入った。

Both the teachers and the students (　　　) (p　　　) with the school's new gymnasium.

(b) 法的な契約書において、一つ一つの言葉は明確な定義を持つべきだ。

Every single word should (　　　) a clear (d　　　) in legal contracts.

(c) 夕食に必要なものを持って、私は支払いカウンターへと進んだ。

I proceeded to the checkout counter with (w　　) I (　　　) for dinner.

(d) サムの楽しい人柄と上手なコミュニケーション・スキルは、彼をとても人気者にしている。

Sam's (p　　　) personality and good communication skills have (　　　) him very popular.

(e) 投票者は新しい大統領を選出することで、現職大統領への不満を表した。

Voters (e　　　) their disapproval of the President by (c　　　) a new one.

Unit 14 Psychology

15歳も50歳も大変

It's Not Easy Being 15 or 50

15歳前後と50歳ごろは、ともに変化の時期だ。前者は少年から大人への移行期であり、後者では体力の衰えを感じ始め、精神的に不安定になることもある。また、15歳前後と50歳ごろは別れの時期でもある。子どもは大学に行ったり働き始めて家を去り、そのことが原因で両親は"空の巣症候群"(empty nest syndrome) と言われる抑うつ的な気分になることがある。

Keywords

本文に使われている次の語句の意味としてもっとも適切なものを a～j から選びなさい。

1. (l.6) transition
2. (l.7) undergo
3. (l.8) emotional
4. (l.10) lead to
5. (l.12) separation
6. (l.16) adjust to
7. (l.18) refer to ... as
8. (l.18) syndrome
9. (l.21) rebellion
10. (l.23) rebel

a. 別れ、別離；独立、分離
b. 反抗、反逆；反乱、暴動
c. 症候群
d. 移行、変遷、変化
e. 感情的な；感情に訴える
f. を経験する；を受ける
g. 反抗する、反発する
h. ～に適応する、順応する
i. ～につながる、をもたらす
j. …を～と呼ぶ

1. (　　)
2. (　　)
3. (　　)
4. (　　)
5. (　　)
6. (　　)
7. (　　)
8. (　　)
9. (　　)
10. (　　)

It's Not Easy Being 15 or 50

The numbers "fifteen" and "fifty" sound very similar—and there are also similarities between the ages 15 and 50. This might seem surprising because a fifteen year-old is a teenager, while a fifty-year-old is a person in middle age. So what are the points in common?

The main similarity is that the period of life around the age of 15 and 50 are both times of transition. In the case of the teenager, it is a transition to adulthood. This is a period when a person undergoes many physical and emotional changes. (A) the same is true of the middle-aged person. Around the age of 50, men and women begin to notice that they do not have as much energy as before, (B) this physical change at middle age often leads to emotional problems, too.

Both 15 and 50 can also be times of "separation." In the case of teenagers, this is a time when they are developing their independence, (C) soon they will leave home to begin university or start working. This transition to a new life can be difficult and stressful, which is one reason why teenagers often argue with their parents. (D) their parents also have to adjust to the independence of not having their children at home. This difficult situation when children leave home is referred to as the "empty nest" syndrome. Parents have a hard time adjusting to this situation, which often happens around the time they are 50.

Everyone knows that the teenage years are a period of rebellion. Many teenagers feel like their parents do not understand their feelings, and as a result they often rebel against their parents. But a middle-aged person around 50 quite often has a similar feeling of wanting to rebel against the situation they are in. That age can be a time when a person feels stress from the heavy responsibilities of work and family life. Around the age of 50, a person sometimes will want to escape these responsibilities and live a freer life.

These are some of the reasons why 15- and 50-year-olds are more similar than most people imagine.

(355 words)

Notes: empty nest syndrome: 空の巣症候群（子どもが家を巣立つ頃に親がかかる抑うつ的な症状）

Unit 14 Phsycology

Exercises

1 本文中の空所（ A),(B),(C),(D ）には "and" または "but" が入る。and が入るときは①を、but が入るときは②を次の空欄に書き入れなさい。なお、文頭に来る文字も小文字で表している。

(A) _____
(B) _____
(C) _____
(D) _____

> ① and
> ② but

2 本文全体のトピックセンテンス（主題文）を探して、該当する英文に下線を引きなさい。

3 質問を読み、正しい答を (A) ～ (D) の中から選びなさい。

Question 1

What is the article's main point about the ages 15 and 50?

(A) It is much harder to be 50 than to be 15.
(B) People who are 50 shouldn't act like 15-year-olds.
(C) People do not change very much during their lives.
(D) Both ages are times when a person often faces difficulties.

Question 2

Why is age 50 often a period of "separation"?

(A) Parents have to pay for university.
(B) It is often a time to begin a new job.
(C) Around that time children leave the home.
(D) Children often argue a lot with their parents.

It's Not Easy Being 15 or 50

4 次の英文は本文の内容に関するものである。本文の内容に一致する場合はTを、一致しない場合はFを下線部に記入しなさい。

(a) The transition to adulthood is stressful to the 50-year-old.
　_____

(b) "Empty nest" syndrome can be difficult for children.
　_____

(c) Like a teenager, 50-year-olds often feel rebellious.
　_____

5 a. に続く b. c. d. の英文を正しく並べ替えて本文の要約文を完成させ、正しい順序を下線部に記入しなさい。また、空欄（ A),(B),(C) に入る最も適切な語句を①～③の中から選びなさい。なお、文頭に来る文字も小文字で表している。

a. The ages 15 and 50 might seem very different, but (A) there are some similarities.
_____

b. (B), they often want to rebel against that situation.

c. (C), a 50-year-old often feels stress about the situation he or she is in.

d. Both ages are a time of many emotional and physical changes.
_____

e. It is surprising how many similarities there are between the two ages.

正しい順序　a → _____ → _____ → _____ → e

(A) _____　(B) _____　(C) _____

> ① in fact
> ② like a teenager
> ③ as a result

Unit 14 Phsycology

6 空欄に適切な単語を書き入れて英訳文を完成させなさい。アルファベットが与えられている場合はその文字で始めること。

(a) すべての新入社員は実際に仕事を始める前に、全般的な研修プログラムを受ける。

All new (e   ) (u   ) a comprehensive training program before they actually start work.

(b) 販売部門が発展させたプロジェクトが、会社の大きな成功につながった。

The project (d   ) by the sales team (l) to great success at the company.

(c) 調査の結果は以下の段落に説明されている。

The (r) of the survey is (e   ) in the following paragraph.

(d) このように多くの無信仰な人たちが特別な休日に教会に行くとは驚きだ。

It is (s   ) how many nonbelievers go to church ( ) special holidays.

(e) 外国を旅行している間は、できるだけ多く現地の人とコミュニケーションをとるようにしなさい。

Try to communicate (   ) local people as (   ) as possible while traveling abroad.

Unit 15 Sports

カーリング・ストーンのトリビア

Curling Stones

カーリングは氷の上で行われるウィンタースポーツ。日本は最近でこそ成績が振るわないが、2002年のソストレイク・オリンピックで7位に入賞し、一躍その名が知れ渡った。現在、世界中の多くの国で行われているが、じつは、使用されるストーンはほとんどがイギリスのスコットランド産とウェールズ産の2種類の花崗岩である。ストーンは氷の上でぶつかり合うので、強度、滑りやすさ、耐水性などが要求される。

Keywords

本文に使われている次の語句の意味としてもっとも適切なものを a~j から選びなさい。

1.	(l.5) quarry [kwɔ́(ː)ri]	a. 花崗岩	1. ( )
2.	(l.8) concentric circles	b. 石切り場；(石)を切り出す	2. ( )
3.	(l.9) collision	c. 同心円	3. ( )
4.	(l.9) granite [grǽnət]	d. 衝突	4. ( )
5.	(l.11) withstand	e. ～を遡る	5. ( )
6.	(l.14) uninhabited	f. ～に耐える [持ちこたえる]	6. ( )
7.	(l.16) trace back	g. を吸収する	7. ( )
8.	(l.17) non-porous	h. を支配する	8. ( )
9.	(l.26) dominate	i. 無人の	9. ( )
10.	(blank) absorb	j. 水や空気を通さない	10. ( )

Unit 15 Sports

Curling has gained increased world-wide popularity since debuting as a Winter Olympic sport in 1998. Today over forty nations compete on some sort of international level. Yet, despite the sport's global flavor, most of the world's curling stones come from one of only two places—special curling stone quarries located in Scotland and Wales.

The stone is a major key to success in curling. The goal of the sport is to slide the stone down a sheet of ice and place it closest to the center of four concentric circles. The route to the center is typically blocked by other stones, often resulting in collisions. The stones are made of granite and by rule must weigh between 17 and 20 kilograms. They must be smooth enough (A) easily over the ice and durable enough to withstand repeated contact with other stones.

By far, the largest percentage of curling stones are quarried on a small, uninhabited island off the coast of Scotland called "Ailsa Craig". This is fitting as Scotland is the traditional home of curling and has a proud curling history that can be traced back over 500 years. Granite from Ailsa Craig is non-porous and is thus slow (B) water, a feature that enables it to slide smoothly over the ice. This is why Ailsa Craig has been the prime source for quality curling stones for over 150 years.

However, only one company—Kays of Scotland—has the right (C) granite from Ailsa Craig. This has led Kays' chief business rival, Canada Curling Stone, to take stones from a different quarry, one near the village of Trefor in Wales. This granite is also of high quality and is perhaps even tougher than that of Ailsa Craig, which means Trefor stones can withstand more impact. Yet, the Ailsa Craig stones still slide somewhat more efficiently.

These two spots—Ailsa Craig and Trefor—dominate the sport of curling. Not only do curling teams compete on the ice but these two quarries also compete to produce the best curling stones in the world.

(344 words)

Curling Stones

Exercises

1 本文中の空欄（ A ），（ B ），（ C ）に入る語句として最も適切なものを下の①～③の中から選びなさい。

(A) _____
(B) _____
(C) _____

① to absorb
② to take
③ to slide

2 本文全体のトピックセンテンス（主題文）を探して、該当する英文に下線を引きなさい。

3 質問を読み、正しい答を (A) ～ (D) の中から選びなさい。

Question 1

This passage focuses on what point in regards to the sport of curling?

(A) That most of the world's curling stones come from one of only two locations.
(B) That the history of curling is closely connected to Scotland.
(C) That the goal of curling is to accurately slide a stone over a sheet of ice.
(D) That Aisla Craig produces non-porous granite for curling stones.

Question 2

According to this passage, what two features are necessary for good curling stones?

(A) Such stones must be from Ailsa Craig or Trefor.
(B) Such stones must be strong enough to withstand collisions and must be able to slide readily over ice.
(C) Such stones must come from one of only two companies.
(D) Such stones must slide down a sheet of ice and come close to the center of four concentric circles.

Unit 15   Sports

4 次の英文は本文の内容に関するものである。本文の内容に一致する場合はTを、一致しない場合はFを下線部に記入しなさい。

(a) The residents of Aisla Craig are proud of their famous granite.
　　 _____

(b) Kays of Scotland is the sole company taking granite from Ailsa Craig.
　　 _____

(c) Granite from Trefor may be stronger than that from Ailsa Craig.
　　 _____

5 a. に続く b. c. d. の英文を正しく並べ替えて本文の要約文を完成させ、正しい順序を下線部に記入しなさい。また、空欄（ A),(B),(C) に入る最も適切な語句を①〜③の中から選び、必要に応じて正しい活用形に変化させ書き入れなさい。

a. Curling has gained much popularity recently and over 40 nations compete at the international level.

b. Aisla Craig granite has been (　A　) for curling stones for over 150 years and can be quarried by only one company, Kays of Scotland.

c. Kays' rival, Canada Curling Stone, (　B　) its granite from Trefor.

d. Yet, curling stones themselves mostly come from only two places in the world, quarries on an island off Scotland (　C　) Ailsa Craig and a quarry in Wales near the village of Trefor.

e. Stones from these two quarries dominate the sport of curling.

　　正しい順序　a → _____ → _____ → _____ → e

　　(A) _____　(B) _____　(C) _____

　　　① call
　　　② use
　　　③ take

6 空欄に適切な単語を書き入れて英訳文を完成させなさい。アルファベットが与えられている場合はその文字で始めること。

(a) 修士号をとるために勉強できるが、学士号を取得してからだ。

You can only study for a Master's Degree (a   ) (g   ) a Bachelor's Degree.

(b) サラは兄のマイクと、両親の関心を引こうと張り合っている。

Sarah (c   ) (w   ) her older brother Mike for their parents' attention.

(c) その映画の筋は、本のそれと若干変わっている。

The story of the movie varies somewhat (f   ) (t   ) of the book.

(d) 断然、年金基金への最良の投資時期はあなたが若い時だ。

(   ) (f   ), the best time to invest in a pension fund is when you are young.

(f) ケイトはブレーキを何度もかけたが、車は氷の上を滑り続けた。

Kate pressed the brakes many times but the car (c   ) (s   ) on the ice.

Active Training for Reading and Writing through 15 Topics

読む力・書く力をつける
15トピックのアクティブ・トレーニング

編著者	マイケル・シャワティ
	トム・ディロン
	西 谷 恒 志
発行者	山 口 隆 史

発 行 所　㈱音羽書房鶴見書店

〒113-0033　東京都文京区本郷 4-1-14
TEL 03-3814-0491
FAX 03-3814-9250
URL: http://www.otowatsurumi.com
e-mail: info@otowatsurumi.com

2016年 3 月 1 日　初版発行
2020年 4 月 1 日　4 刷発行

組版・装幀　ほんのしろ
印刷・製本　（株）シナノ
■ 落丁・乱丁本はお取り替えいたします。

EC-063